eura
favourites

Wendy Hutton

All-time Eurasian favourites like Curry Devil,
Pork Vindaloo and Shepherd's Pie make this an indispensable
book for every kitchen. Stunning photographs and
easy-to-follow recipes will soon have you serving up a wonderful
array of Eurasian dishes to tantalise your tastebuds!

PERIPLUS

Introduction

One of the most intriguing cuisines of Asia is also the least known, even though it is found all the way from India, Sri Lanka and Myanmar to Malaysia, Singapore, Indonesia, Vietnam, Macau and the Philippines.

Eurasian food is the original East-West cuisine, a blending of European and Asian ingredients and cooking styles which began four centuries ago when the Portuguese colonised Goa on India's west coast, and took local women as brides. The Portuguese spread eastwards to Malacca and to Macau, followed over the centuries by the Spanish, British, Dutch and French, all of whom had varying degrees of influence on the people and the cuisine of their Asian colonies.

The beginning of Eurasian cuisine was a story of substitution, such as using coconut milk instead of European cream, or preserved Chinese sausage instead of spicy Portuguese *chorizo*. Traditional Western dishes were found too bland for Eurasian palates, so spices and chillies were added, while some European ingredients (such as Worcestershire sauce, vinegar and mustard) were found to make a magical difference to many Asian recipes.

And so it went, a constant evolution in Eurasian kitchens around Asia, as well as the spread of many Eurasian recipes from one country to another. For example, Goan recipes were taken to the Portuguese colony of Macau; Anglo-Indian dishes spread to Malacca and Penang in Malaysia, and Sri Lankan Eurasians (Burghers) brought their special recipes to Singapore.

With the end of the colonial era (which came much earlier in some countries than others), the cuisine of the Eurasians is slowly disappearing, or becoming more and more a mixture of several Asian styles with very little Western influence remaining. This is particularly true in places like Malaysia and Singapore, where the Eurasian willingness to experiment and adapt has led to a mingling of Malay, Chinese and Indian ingredients, sometimes without any Western influence whatsoever.

The recipes in this book are chosen to reflect that unique blending of East and West which makes Eurasian cuisine so hard to define, yet so appealing to all. Sometimes spicy, always flavourful, with subtle differences reflecting centuries of history, here is a sampling of some of the best Eurasian food.

Important Ingredients

Candlenuts are waxy straw-coloured nuts that are ground and roasted to add texture and flavour to some dishes; substitute raw macadamia nuts or raw cashews.

Chinchalok is a distinctly Peranakan condiment made of fermented shrimp.

Chick pea flour is known as *besan* in India, where it is widely used as a thickener and to flavour stews and other dishes. It is available in stores specializing in Indian ingredients.

Chillies range in size from the commonly used and relatively mild large red (ripe) or green (unripe) finger-length chillies to tiny bird's-eye chillies that provide much more heat. Dried chillies are often used for the brighter red colour

they give to cooked dishes, and for their smoky aroma.

Coconut milk is commonly used in Asian sauces and desserts. If using fresh or frozen coconut, add 125 ml ($^1/_2$ cup) water to about 750 ml (3 cups) of freshly grated coconut. Squeeze and strain the mixture to obtain **thick coconut milk**; skim off the thick portion that rises to the top for **coconut cream**. Add 625 ml ($2^1/_2$ cups) water to the coconut and squeeze again to obtain **thin coconut milk**. Canned or packet concentrated coconut milk is widely available in supermarkets; use without diluting as coconut cream, or dilute according to instructions for thick or thin coconut milk.

Chinese shrimp sauce (*hay koh*) is a black, pungent, molasses-like seasoning made of fermented prawns, salt, sugar and thickeners.

It is used as a sauce or a dip. It is sometimes labelled as *petis* and is unrelated to *belachan*.

Chye sim, also known as choy sum or Chinese Flowering Cabbage, is a leafy green vegetable with crisp crunchy stems. Available in supermarkets in Asia, **chye sim** is now increasingly available in Western countries too. Substitute any other leafy greens.

Coriander is a pungent herb and spice plant that is essential in Southeast Asian cooking. **Coriander leaves**, also known as cilantro, are sold in small bunches with the roots still intact. They are used as a herb and a garnish. Small, round coriander seeds are slightly citrussy in fragrance and are used whole or ground in curry pastes and spice mixes.

Cumin seeds are pale brown to black and usually partnered with coriander seeds in basic spice mixes. They impart an intense, earthy flavour to foods and are often dry-roasted or flash-cooked in oil to intensify their flavour, which is often likened to liquorice.

Daikon radish is a large root vegetable also known as white radish or *lobak*. They are juicy and bland in flavour and can grow to a length of 40 cm (15 in) or more. Choose firm and heavy daikons without any bruises on them. Scrub or peel the skin before you grate or slice the flesh.

Galangal (*lengkuas*) is a very fragrant root belonging to the ginger family. It imparts a distinctive

flavour to many dishes. Look for young, pinkish galangal as it is more tender. Always peel and slice the root before grinding.

Gammon is a form of cured bacon rolled into a joint. It is often boiled or baked. Substitute back bacon or Canadian bacon.

Hot sausage, also known as chorizo, is popular in Goa and Macau; substitute Italian hot sausage or any chilli-hot salami.

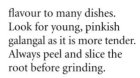

Lap cheong, or dried Chinese sausage, is perfumed with rose-flavoured wine. Generally sold in pairs, these sausages keep without refrigeration and are sliced and cooked with other ingredients rather than eaten on their own. They should not be eaten raw. Substitute any sweet, dried sausage or meat jerky.

Lemongrass (*serai*), also known as citronella, is a

lemon-scented stem which grows in clumps and is an important ingredient in curries and sauces. Use only the thicker bottom third of the lemongrass stem. Remove and discard the dry outer leaves and use only the tender inner part of the plant.

Lemongrass is available fresh, frozen or dried; fresh lemongrass is preferable because of its stronger aroma and flavour.

Mustard seeds are small brownish-black seeds that are commonly used in south Indian cooking, imparting a nutty flavour to dishes.

Paprika is made from mild red peppers that are dried and ground to produce a spice used to flavour and add color to Mediterranean dishes. It is sold in small tins and packets in the spice section of most supermarkets.

Semolina is the ground core of endosperm of durum wheat grains and has a bland flavour and slightly coarse texture. Coarse semolina is used in the recipes in this book, and makes a crunchy coating for fried foods. Finer semolina may be used also. Semolina, both coarse and fine, is used in many Indian sweets and some bread and also is used to make pasta.

Shrimp paste is commonly available in two forms. *Belachan* is the Malay name for dried shrimp paste. Several types are sold, ranging from very moist and black in colour to the light brown, crumbly shrimp paste popular in Malacca. Shrimp paste should be toasted before being used by either dry-frying in a pan, or by placing the *belachan* on the back of a spoon or tip of a knife and toasting it above a flame, or wrapping it in foil and grilling it.

Star anise is a dried brown pod with 8 woody petals, each with a shiny black seed inside. It has the flavour of cinnamon and aniseed. Use whole as a flavouring and discard before eating.

Tamarind juice is made from dried tamarind pulp that is soaked in water, squeezed and then strained to provide a sour, fragrant juice added to many sauces and curries. Soak 1 table-spoon of tamarind pulp in 60 ml ($^1/_4$ cup) warm water,

then mash and strain the mixture to obtain the juice.

Wood ear fungus is a favourite ingredient in Chinese cuisine. Having very little flavour, it is added to dishes for their crunchy texture and to make a fine filling. Dried wood ear fungus is available in plastic packets in most Asian supermarkets and comes in small, crinkly sheets. Soak dried wood ear fungus in water until soft before using and it swells up to many times its original size. Wash well and discard any hard patch that may be growing in the centre of the mature fungus.

Light soy sauce   Black soy sauce

Soy sauce is available in several forms. Light and dark soy sauces are used in this book. Light or "regular" soy is saltier, less malty in flavour and thinner than black soy sauce. Chinese brands of black soy sauce are sometimes labelled "superior sauce".

Meat-filled Buns (Pang Susi)

1 teaspoon sugar
115 ml ($1/_3$ cup plus
  2 tablespoons) milk
30 g butter
$1^1/_2$ teaspoons instant
  yeast
1 egg yolk
185 g ($1^1/_2$ cups) flour,
  sifted
$1/_2$ teaspoon salt
$1/_2$ sweet potato, boiled
  and mashed

Filling
1 tablespoon oil
1 clove garlic, smashed
  and chopped
1 small onion, finely
  chopped
200 g (7 oz) lean minced
  beef or pork
2 teaspoons soy sauce
1 teaspoon black soy
  sauce
$1/_2$ teaspoon coriander
  powder
$1/_4$ teaspoon salt
$1/_4$ teaspoon sugar
$1/_2$ teaspoon freshly
  ground black pepper
$1/_4$ cup (60 ml) water
1 tablespoon chopped
  spring onions

Glaze
1 egg yolk
3 tablespoons milk
1 teaspoon caster sugar

1 Put the sugar, milk and butter into a small saucepan and heat gently, stirring to dissolve the butter. When the liquid is lukewarm, transfer to a small bowl, sprinkle in the yeast and leave until frothy, about 10 minutes. Put the flour and salt in a mixing bowl, making a well in the centre. Add the yeast mixture and the egg yolk, stirring to make a dough. Knead on a floured board until smooth, 3–4 minutes. Return to the bowl and knead in the sweet potato. Transfer to a floured board and knead until smooth and pliable, adding a little more flour if needed so that the dough is not sticky. Cover and leave in a warm place until double in size, 30–40 minutes.

2 Make the Filling while the dough is rising. Heat the oil in a wok. Add the garlic and onion and stir-fry until golden brown, 2–3 minutes. Add the meat, both soy sauces, coriander and salt and pepper and stir-fry over medium heat for 5 minutes. Add the water and stir-fry over low heat until the mixture is dry, about 3 minutes. Stir in the spring onions and transfer to a bowl to cool.

3 Turn the dough onto a floured board and cut into 10 pieces. Flatten each portion to make an oval 10–12 cm long. Put 1 heaped tablespoon of the meat in the centre of each oval. Pinch the edges together tightly to enclose the Filling. Put the sealed side down on a greased baking tray. Cover with a clean cloth and leave until double in size, about 30 minutes.

4 Combine the ingredients for the Glaze then brush it generously over the top of the buns. Bake at 190°C (375°F) until golden brown, about 20 minutes. Remove from the oven and brush again with the Glaze. Serve warm or at room temperature.

Serves 4
Preparation time: 25 mins + $1^1/_4$ hours rising time
Cooking time: **35 mins**

Spicy Anglo-Indian Fried Bread

8 slices dry or lightly
  toasted white bread
Ghee or oil for frying

Masala
150 g (1^1/$_2$ cups) freshly
  grated coconut
1 onion, sliced
1^1/$_2$ tablespoons chickpea
  flour (*besan*)
1 tablespoon chopped
  coriander leaves
Ground black pepper
^{1}/$_2$–^{3}/$_4$ teaspoon salt
^{1}/$_2$ teaspoon cumin
  powder
^{1}/$_2$ teaspoon chilli powder

1 Place all the Masala ingredients in a blender or food
processor and blend to a smooth paste.
2 Put one-eighth of the mixture in the centre of each slice
of bread, spreading it to the edges and pressing down with
a spatula to make it adhere.
3 Heat a little ghee or oil in a frying pan (preferably non-
stick) and fry the slices of bread over moderate heat for
about 3 to 4 minutes, until golden brown underneath.
Turn and cook the other side.
4 Cut into triangles and serve hot, or top each slice with
a poached or fried egg.

*If freshly grated or frozen fresh coconut is not avail-
able, use 90 g (1^1/$_4$ cups) desiccated coconut moistened
with warm water.*

Serves 4
Preparation time: **10 mins**
Cooking time: **10–15 mins**

Crab and Potato Cakes

200 g (7 oz) cooked
  crabmeat
2 medium potatoes,
  peeled, boiled and
  mashed
1 egg yolk
1 teaspoon salt
White pepper
1 teaspoon soy sauce
1 teaspoon lemon juice
2 tablespoons finely
  chopped spring onions
2 tablespoons finely
  chopped coriander leaves
60 g ($^1/_2$ cup) plain flour
1 egg, lightly beaten
100 g (1 cup) breadcrumbs
Oil for shallow frying
60 ml ($^1/_4$ cup) bottled
  chilli sauce

1 Flake the crabmeat with your fingers and remove any bits of shell or cartilage. Combine the crabmeat, mashed potatoes, egg yolk, salt, pepper, soy sauce, lemon juice, spring onions and coriander in a bowl, stirring to mix well. Shape into balls about 5 cm (2 in) in diameter, then flatten until about $1^1/_2$ cm ($^2/_3$ in) thick.

2 Sprinkle each cake lightly with flour. Dip into the egg then the breadcrumbs, turning to coat all over. Put the coated crab cakes in a covered container and refrigerate for 30 minutes; this helps prevent the crumbs falling off during frying.

3 Heat about 3 tablespoons of oil in a frying pan (preferably non-stick) and fry the cakes over moderate heat until golden brown on each side.

4 Drain on paper towels and serve with chilli sauce.

Makes 14 crab cakes
Preparation time: **15 mins**
Cooking time: **20 mins (including boiling time)**

Mulligatawny

2 tablespoons oil
1 teaspoon very finely
  chopped ginger
1 teaspoon very finely
  chopped garlic
1 onion, thinly sliced
3 tablespoons chickpea
  flour (*besan*)
1¹/₂–2 tablespoons curry
  powder
1 teaspoon black pepper
¹/₄ teaspoon turmeric
  powder
1 tart green apple, peeled
  and diced
2 medium tomatoes,
  chopped
4 cups (1 litre) chicken
  stock

1 bay leaf
125 g (4 oz) boneless
  chicken breast
1–2 tablespoons cooked
  rice (optional)

Salt to taste
Fresh coriander leaves
  to garnish
1 lime or lemon,
  cut in wedges

1 Heat the oil in a large pan and stir-fry the ginger, garlic
and onion over medium heat until the onion is transparent.
Add the chickpea flour, curry powder, pepper, turmeric,
apple, tomatoes, bay leaf and stock. Bring to a boil, stirring
several times, then lower the heat, cover and simmer for
30 minutes. Add the chicken and simmer for 15 minutes.
2 Discard the bay leaf. Remove the chicken and shred. Set
aside. Blend the soup and return to the pan. Add the rice,
if using, and the chicken and heat. Taste and add salt if
desired. Serve in individual bowls with a sprig of coriander.
Accompany with a wedge of lime or lemon .

Serves 4
Preparation time: **15 mins**
Cooking time: **1 hour**

Potato and Vegetable Soup with Hot Sausage

3–4 potatoes, peeled and
  cubed
5 cups (1$^1/_4$ litres) water
1 large onion, chopped
1–2 cloves garlic, chopped
3–4 teaspoons olive oil
1 teaspoon salt
250 g (8 oz) bok choy
  (mustard cabbage),
  white stems discarded
$^1/_2$ cup finely shredded
  spicy hot sausage,
  (chorizo) or shredded
  hot salami
White pepper to taste

1 Put the potatoes, water, onion, garlic, oil and salt in a saucepan and bring to a boil. Cover and simmer until the potatoes are soft. Blend until smooth. This basic mixture can be set aside for a few hours or even refrigerated for a day or two until the soup is required.

2 To finish the soup, shred the green leaves of the bok choy very finely. Reheat the potato mixture, then add the shredded bok choy and hot sausage.

3 Simmer until the bok choy is tender. Serve the soup sprinkled with white pepper and serve hot with crusty French bread.

Serves 4
Preparation time: **10 mins**
Cooking time: **25 mins**

Rice with Smoked Fish

This Anglo-Indian favourite, also known as *kedgeree*, was a popular dish in 19th century Britain. It can still be found in India. The original *kichri* is an ancient recipe of buttered rice and lentils, topped with fried onions; this more substantial version adds smoked fish, peas and hard-boiled eggs.

250 g (8 oz) smoked fish (haddock, mackerel, cod, trout or salmon)
250 ml (1 cup) milk
20 g (1 tablespoon) ghee or butter
1 onion, halved length-wise, thinly sliced
1 green chilli, thinly sliced
1 clove garlic, smashed and finely chopped
1 teaspoon grated fresh ginger
5-cm (2-in) cinnamon stick
400 g (2 cups) uncooked rice, washed and drained
1 teaspoon salt
$^1/_2$ teaspoon turmeric
750 ml (3 cups) boiling water
180 g (1 cup) frozen green peas, defrosted
2 hard-boiled eggs, chopped
Sprig of parsley to garnish, (optional)
Crispy Fried Shallots, to garnish (optional)

1 Heat the ghee in a large pan and gently stir-fry the onion over medium heat until it browns, 7–8 minutes. Add the chilli, garlic, ginger and cinnamon and stir-fry for 3 minutes. Add the rice and turmeric, stirring for 1 minute to coat with ghee.

2 Add the salt and boiling water. Stir over high heat until boiling rapidly, then reduce the heat, cover and simmer the rice until all the water is absorbed, about 5 minutes. Remove the lid and wipe it dry. Add the peas, stir, cover and reduce the heat to low. Simmer for 10 minutes.

3 While the rice is cooking, put the smoked fish in a small saucepan and add the milk. Bring to a boil, lower the heat and simmer until cooked, about 5 minutes. Remove the fish, drain and flake it with a fork. Set aside.

4 When the rice is cooked, add the fish and eggs to the pan and stir gently to combine. Transfer to a serving dish and garnish with parsley and fried shallots, if using. Serve hot.

*To make **Crispy Fried Shallots**, peel and thinly slice 8 shallots. Heat 60 ml ($^1/_4$ cup) oil in a wok until the oil is just warm. Add the shallots and cook very slowly, stirring several times, until golden brown, about 5 minutes. Remove the shallots and drain on a paper towel; they will become crisp as they cool.*
Store in an air-tight jar. Ready-made fried shallots are also sold in packets at markets and grocery shops.

Serves 4
Preparation time: **10 mins**
Cooking time: **30 mins**

Mixed Festive Rice

Stock

- 2 whole chicken legs (thighs and drumsticks), skin removed
- 200 g (7 oz) streaky pork, sliced
- 1 1/4 litres (5 cups) water
- 1 onion, quartered
- 5-cm (2-in) cinnamon stick
- 1 star anise pod
- 4 cloves
- 1/4 teaspoon peppercorns
- 1 teaspoon salt

Rice Mixture

- 20 g (1 tablespoon) butter
- 5-cm (2-in) cinnamon stick
- 4 cardamom pods, slit
- 4 cloves
- 1 onion, finely chopped
- 1 1/2 teaspoons garlic, very finely chopped
- 1 1/2 teaspoons finely chopped ginger
- 400 g (2 cups) uncooked rice, washed and drained
- 2 tablespoons tomato paste
- 1 teaspoon salt

Garnishes

- 4 frankfurters, cut in half, or 12 cocktail sausages, fried
- 1 hard-boiled egg, sliced
- 1 large tomato, sliced or 12 cherry tomatoes
- 1 slice dry or lightly toasted white bread, diced and fried until golden brown, or croutons
- 2 tablespoons slivered almonds, lightly toasted
- 1 tablespoon raisins
- Sprigs of parsley or fresh coriander leaves

1 To make the Stock, put the chicken and pork into a large saucepan with the water, onion, cinnamon, cardamom pods, star anise, cloves, peppercorns and salt. Bring to a boil, cover and simmer for 15 minutes. Strain and reserve the Stock. Cut the chicken and pork into bite-sized pieces and set aside.

2 To prepare the Rice Mixture, heat the butter in a large saucepan. Stir-fry the cinnamon, cardamom and cloves for 1 minute, then add the onion, garlic and ginger, and stir-fry over medium heat until the onion turns transparent, 2–3 minutes. Add the rice and stir gently for 1 minute, then stir in the tomato paste.

3 Reheat 3 1/2 cups of the reserved Stock then add it to the Rice Mixture with the reserved chicken and pork. Raise the heat and bring to a boil. Partially cover the pan and simmer until the rice is dry, about 5 minutes. Cover and cook over minimum heat for 10 minutes. Wipe the lid dry, fluff up the rice with a fork, turn off the heat and let the rice stand for 10 minutes.

4 Place the rice into a large serving bowl. Arrange the frankfurters, egg, tomato, fried bread, almonds, raisins and parsley neatly on the rice and serve hot, accompanied by a salad (such as cucumber and pineapple) and a hot sambal or pickle.

Serves 4–6
Preparation time: **20 mins**
Cooking time: **45–50 mins**

Birthday Noodles

2 tablespoons oil
3 shallots, finely sliced
1 clove garlic, smashed
and finely chopped
1 tablespoon salted fer-
mented soy beans (*tau
cheo*), mashed, or miso
150 g small fresh prawns,
peeled and deveined
$1/_2$ teaspoon salt
$1/_2$ teaspoon sugar
100 g ($3^1/_3$ oz) *choy sum*
(*chye sim*), cut in
lengths
100 g (1 heaped cup)
bean sprouts, tops and
tails removed
500 g (1 lb) fresh yellow
wheat noodles (mee),
rinsed and drained

Chicken Stock
1 large chicken leg
(thigh and drumstick),
skin removed
500 ml (2 cups) water
2 shallots, chopped
1 clove garlic, chopped
2 teaspoons black soy
sauce
$1/_2$ teaspoon salt
$1/_2$ teaspoon sugar
5-cm (2-in) cinnamon
stick
2 cloves

Garnishes
1 egg, cooked to make a
thin omelette, finely
sliced
$1/_2$ small cucumber,
peeled and deseeded,
flesh grated
1 large red chilli, sliced
1 tablespoon Crispy Fried
Shallots (page 12)
Sprigs of coriander
leaves
4 lime wedges

Serves 4
Preparation time: **20 mins**
Cooking time: **45 mins**

1 To make the Chicken Stock, put all the ingredients in a medium saucepan, bring to a boil, cover, lower the heat and simmer until the chicken is tender, about 30 minutes. Cut the chicken meat into strips. Strain the Chicken Stock into a bowl and set aside

2 Heat the oil in a wok and add the shallots and garlic. Stir-fry until transparent, then add the salted soy beans and stir-fry for 1 minute. Add the prawns and stir-fry just until they change colour, then sprinkle with the salt and sugar. Add the cabbage and stir-fry until it starts to soften, about 1 minute. Add the bean sprouts and stir-fry for a few seconds, then add the noodles and chicken.

3 Stir-fry to mix well, then add 1 cup of the reserved Chicken Stock and cook over high heat, stirring frequently, until the stock has been absorbed and the noodles are cooked, about 3 minutes. Transfer the noodles to a large serving dish and sprinkle the Garnish on top. Squeeze with lime juice to taste.

Chicken Stock can be substituted with one can of chicken stock and $1/_2$ cup water, or 1 small stock cube with 1 cup water.

Spicy Whole Fried Fish

4 small mackerel or other whole fish such as flounder, bream or snapper, scaled, cleaned and gutted
Oil for shallow frying
2 tomatoes, sliced (optional)
1 large onion, sliced (optional)
Sprigs of fresh coriander leaves (optional)
Vinegar to taste
Salt to taste

Spice Mixture
4–5 dried chillies, deeseeded and cut into lengths
2 tablespoons coconut or rice vinegar
1 heaped tablespoon dried tamarind pulp
$1/_2$ teaspoon cumin
4 cloves
$1/_4$ teaspoon peppercorns
2 cm ($3/_4$ in) fresh ginger, chopped
3 cloves garlic, chopped
1 onion, chopped and fried in a little oil until golden brown
$1/_2$ teaspoon turmeric
2 teaspoons sugar
1 teaspoon salt

1 Prepare the Spice Mixture by soaking the chillies in vinegar until very soft, about 30 minutes. Drain the chillies, reserving the vinegar. Pick over the tamarind, discarding any skin, fibres and seeds; this should yield about 1 teaspoon of cleaned pulp.

2 Heat the cumin, cloves and peppercorns in a dry pan until fragrant, shaking the pan and taking care not to burn. Grind to a powder in a spice grinder or blender. Add the reserved vinegar, ginger, garlic, fried onion, turmeric, sugar and salt and process to a smooth paste. This Spice Mixture can be refrigerated in a covered container for several hours until finishing the recipe.

3 Use a sharp, pointed knife to cut a pocket along each side of the backbone of the fish, cutting almost to the edge of the underneath of the fish so that there is plenty of room for the Spice Mixture. Divide the Spice Mixture between the pockets and push in firmly.

4 Heat the oil for shallow-frying in a large skillet and fry the fish over moderate heat, turning until golden brown on both sides and cooked through, about 8 minutes for smaller fish, 20–25 minutes for a large fish. Alternatively, brush both sides of the fish with a little oil and grill until cooked.

5 Serve with a salad of sliced tomatoes, onion rings and sprigs of fresh coriander leaves, sprinkled with a little vinegar and salt.

Serves 4
Preparation time: **15 mins + 30 mins soaking**
Cooking time: **30 mins**

Portuguese-style Chilli Fish Stew

4 white fish cutlets or
fillets, each about 150 g
(5 oz), dried on paper
towels
6 ripe tomatoes, peeled
and diced
1 onion, thinly sliced
4–5 large green chillies,
halved lengthwise, or
1–1$^1/_2$ teaspoons
chilli powder
250 ml (1 cup) water
1 tablespoon tomato paste
1 tablespoon vinegar or
lemon juice
1 teaspoon salt
50 g (2 $^1/_2$ table-
spoons)butter

1 Cut the fish into rectangular fillets or large chunks.
2 Put all the ingredients except the fish into a wide
saucepan that will hold the fish in one layer and bring to
a boil. Simmer uncovered, stirring from time to time,
about 5 minutes.
3 Add the fish and cook until the fish is tender and the
gravy has thickened, turning the pieces of fish after
4 minutes to cook evenly.
4 Serve with rice or crusty French bread.

*Cod or John Dory fillets are ideal for this dish. Any
firm-fleshed fillets such as blue eye or ocean perch
can be substituted*

Serves 4
Preparation time: **10 mins**
Cooking time: **15 mins**

Fried Fish Cutlets with Sambal Chinchalok

1 teaspoon salt
1 teaspoon turmeric
  powder
$^1/_2$ teaspoon chilli powder
4 slices *ikan tenggiri*
  (Spanish mackerel),
  each about 120 g (4 oz),
  or other white firm-
  fleshed fish
60 ml ($^1/_4$ cup) oil

Sambal Chinchalok
4 tablespoons bottled
  chinchalok
3–4 shallots, very thinly
  sliced
1 large red chilli, thinly
  sliced
60 ml ($^1/_4$ cup) lime juice

1 To make the *Sambal Chinchalok*, put all the ingredients in a bowl and toss to mix well. Serve at room temperature; refrigerate any leftover in a covered container for up to 2 days.

2 Prepare the fish by combining the salt, turmeric and chilli in a small bowl. Pat the fish dry on both sides, then sprinkle with the salt mixture. Allow to marinate for 2–3 minutes.

3 Heat the oil in a frying pan and fry the fish over medium heat until golden brown on both sides and cooked through, 6-8 minutes, depending on the thickness of the fish.

4 Drain and serve with steamed rice, *Sambal Chinchalok* and vegetables.

Serves 4
Preparation time: **10–15 mins**
Cooking time: **10 mins**

Sambal Pepper Prawns (Pementa)

60 ml ($^1/_4$ cup) oil
625 ml ($2^1/_2$ cups) water
750 g ($1^1/_2$ lbs) fresh
    prawns, peeled and
    deveined, tails left on
8 ladies' fingers, cut
    diagonally, or 4 small
    slender eggplants,
    halved lengthwise
1 tablespoon tamarind
    pulp, mashed in 60 ml
    ($^1/_4$ cup) warm water,
    squeezed and strained
    to obtain juice
1 teaspoon salt
1–2 teaspoons sugar

Spice Paste
2 teaspoons black
    peppercorns
1 teaspoon cumin
$^1/_2$ teaspoon fennel
3 candlenuts, chopped
6–8 dried chillies, cut in
    lengths, deseeded and
    soaked in hot water
    to soften
8 shallots, chopped
3–4 cloves garlic, chopped
1 stem lemongrass,
    tender inner part of
    bottom third only,
    thinly sliced
1 cm ($^1/_2$ in) fresh
    turmeric, chopped
$^1/_2$ teaspoon dried shrimp
    paste (belachan)

1 To prepare the Spice Paste, toast the pepper, cumin and
fennel seeds lightly in a dry skillet, then grind to a powder
in a spice grinder. Add the remaining ingredients and
process to a smooth paste, adding a little of the oil if
needed to keep the mixture turning.
2 Heat the oil in a saucepan and add the Spice Paste. Stir-
fry over medium heat for 5 minutes. Add 1 cup of the
water, bring to a boil, cover and simmer for 5 minutes.
Add the remaining water, prawns, ladies' fingers, tamarind
juice, salt and 1 teaspoon of the sugar. Bring to a boil and
simmer uncovered until the prawns and ladies' fingers
are cooked. (If using eggplant, simmer for 3 minutes
before adding the prawns and tamarind juice.)
3 Taste and add more sugar and, if preferred, pepper.
Serve with rice, potatoes or bread.

*This dish is also delicious with fish. Use 600 g ($1^1/_4$ lbs)
ikan tenggiri (Spanish mackerel), or stingray in place
of the prawns.*

Serves 4
Preparation time: 25 mins
Cooking time: **15 mins**

Spicy Grilled Chicken

1 fresh chicken, quartered
2 tablespoons olive oil
1 teaspoon garlic, finely chopped
1 tablespoon tomato paste
1 cup (250 ml) coconut milk
1 cup (250 ml) chicken stock
$1/4$ cup (60 ml) white wine
1 teaspoon sesame oil
1 teaspoon smooth peanut butter
$1/2$ teaspoon salt
$1/4$ teaspoon white pepper

Marinade
2 tablespoons crushed chilli
3 teaspoons very finely chopped garlic
1 tablespoon light soy sauce
$1/2$ teaspoon paprika (optional)

1 Combine the Marinade ingredients and rub the
Marinade into the chicken pieces, cover and marinate for
at least 3 hours, or overnight.
2 Heat the oil in a wok and fry the chicken pieces over
medium–high heat, turning to brown all sides. Reduce
the heat slightly, add the garlic and tomato paste, and
stir-fry for 1 minute.
3 Add the coconut milk, chicken stock, wine, sesame oil,
peanut butter, salt and pepper. Bring to a boil, stirring
frequently, then reduce the heat and simmer uncovered,
turning the chicken pieces several times until the chicken
is tender and the sauce is dry. The chicken can now be set
aside until just before it is to be served.
4 Grill the chicken very quickly on a barbecue or under
an oven grill until golden brown on both sides. Serve hot
with crusty French bread or rice and salad.

Serves 4
Preparation time: **15 mins + marinating time**
Cooking time: **1 hour**

Braised Chicken and Potatoes with Olives

1 fresh chicken, cut into
  serving pieces, or 1 kg
  (2 lbs) chicken pieces
1 teaspoon salt
$^{1}/_{2}$ teaspoon freshly
  ground black pepper
1 tablespoon olive oil
2 onions, finely chopped
3 cloves garlic, smashed
  and chopped
2 cm ($^{3}/_{4}$ in) fresh ginger,
  very finely chopped
1 teaspoon turmeric
  powder
1 tablespoon flour
1 large ripe tomato,
  skinned and chopped
1 tablespoon tomato
  ketchup
2 teaspoons
  Worcestershire sauce
250 ml (1 cup) chicken
  stock
250 ml (1 cup) white wine
250 ml (1 cup) thin
  coconut milk
1 bay leaf
8–10 green olives
2–3 medium potatoes,
  peeled and cut into
  chunks
100 g ($3^{1}/_{3}$ oz) hot
  sausage, or salami, thickly
  sliced
Lime or lemon wedges

1 Sprinkle the chicken with salt and a little black pepper.
Heat a wok then add the oil. When hot, add a few chicken
pieces and cook over moderate heat, turning, until brown
on all sides. Remove and drain on paper towels. Continue
until all the chicken is browned.

2 Using the oil remaining in the wok, stir-fry the onion,
garlic and ginger until transparent, then sprinkle in the
turmeric and flour. Stir for 30 seconds, then add the tomato
and stir-fry until it softens, 3–4 minutes.

3 Add the tomato and Worcestershire sauce and a little of
the chicken stock, stirring until the flour is blended, then
add the remaining stock, wine, coconut milk, bay leaves,
olives and potatoes. Bring to a boil, reduce the heat and
let simmer for 10 minutes, stirring frequently.

4 Add the chicken pieces and simmer gently, with the
wok uncovered, for another 10 minutes. Add the sausage
and potatoes and continue simmering until the chicken
and potatoes are tender.

5 Serve garnished with lime or lemon wedges.

*To peel the tomatoes, dip them in rapidly boiling water
for 15–20 seconds. Put under running water until cool
enough to handle. Use a sharp knife to remove core,
then slip off the skin.*

Serves 4
Preparation time: **30 mins**
Cooking time: **45 mins**

Penang-style Fried Chicken

1 whole chicken, cut into serving pieces, or 1 kg (2 lbs) chicken pieces (thighs and breasts)
Oil for deep-frying

Marinade
1 tablespoon coriander, seeds, toasted in a dry pan until fragrant
10 shallots, chopped
2 teaspoons garlic, chopped
1 tablespoon ginger, chopped
8–10 dried chillies, cut in lengths, soaked to soften
3 stems lemongrass, tender inner part of bottom third only, thinly sliced
2 tablespoons soy sauce
1 tablespoon black soy sauce
1 tablespoon lime juice
1 tablespoon sugar
1 teaspoon salt

Dipping Sauce
2 tablespoons Worcestershire sauce
1 tablespoon soy sauce
1 tablespoon sugar
2 teaspoons lime juice
1 teaspoon hot English mustard powder
2 shallots, thinly sliced
1 large red chilli, finely chopped

1 To prepare the Marinade, grind the coriander seeds to a fine powder in a spice grinder, then add the shallots, garlic, ginger, chillies and lemongrass and grind to a smooth paste, adding a little of the soy sauce if needed to keep the mixture turning. Transfer to a bowl and stir in the soy sauces, lime juice, sugar and salt. Add the chicken, stirring to coat with the Marinade. Cover and refrigerate at least 4 hours or overnight, turning several times.
2 To make the Dipping Sauce, combine all the ingredients, mixing well. Set aside for the flavours to meld.
3 Remove the chicken pieces from the bowl and drain on paper towels to remove the liquid. Heat the oil for deep-frying in a wok. When very hot, deep-fry the chicken pieces, a few at a time, until golden brown and cooked through. Drain on paper towels and keep warm while frying the remaining chicken. Alternatively, grill the chicken pieces under high heat, or barbecue until golden brown on both sides and cooked through.
4 Serve hot with the Dipping Sauce.

Serves 4
Preparation time: 25 mins + 4 hours marinating
Cooking time: 10 mins (15–20 if grilling)

Chicken Curry Devil

Made by Eurasians from Sri Lanka to Singapore, Curry Devil was traditionally cooked on Boxing Day to use up leftover meat. A genuine Devil is a lavish dish, worth making only for a large number of guests. This is a simplified Malacca version.

1 fresh chicken, cut into bite-sized portions
1 tablespoon black soy sauce
125 ml ($^1/_2$ cup) oil
2 onions, quartered
750 ml (3 cups) water
2 stems lemongrass, bruised
$1^1/_2$ teaspoons salt
250 g (8 oz) Chinese roast pork (with skin), sliced (optional)
3 potatoes, peeled and quartered
2 tablespoons vinegar
2 teaspoons sugar
1 teaspoon hot English mustard powder

Spice Paste
2 teaspoons brown mustard seeds
12–16 dried chillies, cut into lengths, deseeded and soaked to soften
4 red chillies, sliced
10 shallots
4 cloves garlic,
5-cm (2-in) ginger
3-cm (1-in) galangal,
3 candlenuts

1 Prepare the Spice Paste by processing the mustard seeds in a spice grinder or blender until coarsely ground. Add both lots of chillies, shallots, garlic, ginger, galangal and candlenuts and blend to a smooth paste (in two stages if the spice grinder is small), adding a little of the oil if necessary to keep mixture turning.

2 Put 4 tablespoons of the Spice Paste and the soy sauce in a large bowl and stir to mix well. Add the chicken and mix to coat well with the mixture.

3 Heat a wok, add 60 ml ($^1/_4$ cup) of the oil and heat until very hot. Add the marinated chicken and stir-fry until it changes colour, 3–4 minutes. Remove the chicken pieces and set aside. Add the remaining oil, reduce the heat and stir-fry the remaining Spice Paste and quartered onions over medium heat for 4–5 minutes.

4 Add the water, lemongrass and salt and simmer for 2 minutes, scraping any Spice Paste from the bottom. Add the chicken, cover the wok and simmer, stirring occasionally, for 10 minutes. Add the roast pork, if using, and potatoes, and simmer until cooked, about 20 minutes, stirring occasionally. Combine the vinegar, sugar and mustard in a bowl, then add to the wok, stirring for about 1 minute to mix well.

5 Transfer to a large bowl and serve with steamed white rice.

Serves 4
Preparation time: 30–35 mins
Cooking time: 50 mins

Vegetable, Bean and Pork Stew

This hearty dish of kidney beans and pork, *feijoada*, originated in the once-Portuguese colony of Brazil. Different versions are now found in ex-Portuguese enclaves of Goa and Macau, this Macanese recipe showing definite Chinese influence in the addition of sweet Chinese dried sausages and long white radish.

300 g (2 cups) dried kidney beans
1 tablespoon pork lard or olive oil
2 onions, chopped
2 cloves garlic, minced
500 g (1 lb) pork loin preferably with a little skin and fat, cubed
4 tomatoes, peeled and chopped
1 teaspoon salt, or more to taste
1 teaspoon freshly ground black pepper
125 ml ($1/_2$ cup) white wine
2 carrots, sliced
180 g (6 oz) daikon radish (lobak), halved length-wise, and thinly sliced
4 cabbage leaves, chopped
2 *lap cheong* (dried Chinese sausages), thinly sliced

1 Place the kidney beans in a large saucepan and add $1^1/_2$ litres (6 cups) of water. Bring to a boil, turn off the heat and cover. Let stand for 1 hour. Drain the beans and discard the water, then cover them with fresh water and bring to a boil again. Cover and simmer over medium heat, 30–45 minutes, until soft. Drain, reserving the water.

2 Rinse and dry the pan, then add the lard or oil and heat. Stir-fry the onions over medium heat until they become transparent, about 4 minutes. Add the garlic and stir-fry until fragrant, about 1–2 minutes. Add the pork and stir-fry until it changes colour. Add the tomatoes and cook, stirring several times, until they start to soften. Add the salt, pepper, kidney beans, wine and enough of the reserved water to cover. Bring to a boil, cover and simmer gently until the pork and beans are tender, about 30 minutes, adding a little water if necessary.

3 Add the carrots, radish and cabbage, bring back to the boil, cover and simmer until the vegetables are tender, about 15 minutes. Add the *lap cheong* and heat through for 1–2 minutes, until the *lap cheong* starts to soften. Serve hot with crusty French bread.

Serves 6
Preparation time: 45 mins + 1 hour soaking time for kidney beans
Cooking time: $1^3/_4$ hours

Assam Soy Pork with Shrimp Sauce

65 g (1/4 cup) dried tamarind pulp
185 ml (3/4 cup) warm water
750 g (1 1/2 lbs) pork, preferably with fat and skin left on, cubed
2 tablespoons olive oil
1 tablespoon Chinese shrimp sauce
1 onion, finely diced
2 cloves garlic, minced
1 tablespoon black soy sauce
2–3 tablespoons chopped palm sugar or soft brown sugar
1 red chilli, thinly sliced lengthwise (optional)
2 stalks spring onions, thinly sliced lengthwise (optional)

Marinade

3 cloves garlic, minced
2 bay leaves
1 tablespoon lemon juice
2 teaspoons black soy sauce
2 teaspoons rice wine,

1 Soak the tamarind in warm water for 5 minutes, then mash and strain to obtain tamarind juice. Place the juice into a bowl and add the pork and all the Marinade ingredients, mixing well. Cover and refrigerate at least 4 hours, or overnight. Drain the Marinade from the pork before cooking.

2 Heat 1 tablespoon of the oil in a large saucepan and stir-fry the pork over high heat until golden brown. Remove the pork and set aside. Lower the heat, add the remaining oil and, when hot, add the shrimp sauce and stir-fry until fragrant, about 1 minute. Add the onion and stir-fry for 1 minute, then add the garlic and cook until fragrant, 2–3 minutes.

3 Return the pork to the pan and stir-fry for 1 minute, then add the reserved Marinade, soy sauce and palm sugar, stirring until the sugar dissolves. Cover the pan and simmer gently until the pork is tender and the sauce has thickened. Garnish with red chilli, and spring onion and serve with steamed rice.

Serves 4
Preparation time: **15 mins + marinating time**
Cooking time: **1 1/4 hours**

Fiery Vindaloo Pork Curry

Vindaloo used to be taken on sea voyages by Goan sailors, as it keeps well without refrigeration owing to its low water content and the use of vinegar and spices. Goa is the only place in India where vinegar, introduced by the Portuguese, is used as a souring agent for food. Vindaloo, perfect for lovers of really hot and emphatically flavoured food, is also popular in Malacca.

10 dried chillies, cut in pieces
1/2 cup (125 ml) coconut or rice vinegar
About 700 g (1 1/2 lbs) pork, preferably shoulder, with a little fat, cubed
4 cloves garlic
4 cm (1 1/2 in) ginger
1/2 teaspoon turmeric powder
1 teaspoon salt
1/4 cup (60 ml) oil

Spices

4 teaspoons cumin
4 teaspoons brown mustard seeds
1 teaspoon black peppercorns
2 cardamom pods, slit, or 1/4 teaspoon cardamom powder
4 cloves
1 cm (1/2 in) cinnamon

1 Soak the dried chillies in vinegar until soft, 20–30 minutes. Drain, reserving the vinegar.
2 Put all the Spices in a small pan and dry-roast over low heat, shaking the pan, until fragrant, about 1 minute. Grind to a fine powder in a spice grinder then set aside. Process the garlic, ginger and chillies to make a fine paste. Add a little oil if needed, to keep the mixture turning.
3 Put the pork in a large glass bowl, add the ground Spices, chilli paste, turmeric, salt and vinegar. Mix thoroughly and set aside for at least 4 hours to marinate. The meat can be refrigerated overnight if desired.
4 Heat the oil in a heavy stainless steel or enamelled pan until moderately hot (do not use aluminium as it will react with the vinegar). Drain the meat, reserving the marinade. Stir-fry the meat until it changes colour, add the marinade and cover the pan. Simmer over very low heat, stirring occasionally, until the meat is tender, about 1–1 1/4 hours. Serve with steamed rice.

Serves 6
Preparation time: 30 mins
Cooking time: 1 1/4 hours

Shepherd's Pie

The original British version of this dish usually containes leftover roast lamb, but this popular Eurasian family recipe uses raw minced beef as the basic ingredient, although pork or chicken may be substituted if preferred.

3 tablespoons oil
2 teaspoons garlic, minced
3–4 dried Chinese mushrooms, soaked to soften, stems removed, caps thinly sliced
500 g (1 lb) minced beef
60 g ($^1/_2$ cup) frozen peas, thawed
125 ml ($^1/_2$ cup) water
1 tablespoon oyster sauce
1 tablespoon Worcestershire sauce
2 teaspoons soy sauce
1 teaspoon sugar
$^1/_2$ teaspoon freshly ground black pepper
1 egg, lightly beaten (optional)

Topping
750 g (1$^1/_2$ lbs) potatoes, boiled, peeled and mashed
$^3/_4$ teaspoon salt
$^1/_2$ teaspoon freshly ground black pepper
1 egg yolk (optional)
2 tablespoons butter
250 ml (1 cup) milk, or more if required

1 To prepare the Topping, mix the mashed potatoes with the salt, pepper, egg yolk, butter and enough milk to achieve a creamy texture; the amount of milk required will depend on the texture of the potatoes. Preheat the oven to 180°C (350°F).

2 Heat the oil in a pan. When it is moderately hot, add the garlic and stir-fry for a few seconds, then add the mushrooms and stir-fry for 1 minute. Add the beef and continue stir-frying until it changes colour, about 2–3 minutes. Lower the heat slightly and add the peas. Cook, stirring frequently, for 3 minutes. Add the water, oyster sauce, Worcestershire sauce, soy sauce, sugar and pepper, stirring until the water has been absorbed.

3 Use an oval oven-proof casserole dish about 30 cm long, or a square or rectangular baking dish of a similar capacity. Put the beef mixture in the pan, pressing it down gently. Cover with a layer of the Topping, spreading it evenly with a spatula. Make a criss-cross design on the top with a fork, and brush with the beaten egg if using.

4 Transfer to the preheated oven and cook for 30 minutes. If the Topping has not turned golden brown, place under a hot grill for about 5 minutes. Serve warm.

Serves 4
Preparation time: **40 mins**
Cooking time: **1 hour**

Hearty Oxtail Stew

Oxtail stew is a popular family dish among most Singapore Eurasians, and although there are many different versions, most combine local spices and seasonings with traditional English ingredients, such as Worcestershire sauce.

2 tablespoons oil
2 cloves garlic, minced
3 onions, thinly sliced
8 cm (3 in) cinnamon
  stick
2 star anise pods
6 cloves
1/4 teaspoon peppercorns
1 1/2 kg (3 lbs) oxtail, cut
  in short lengths, fat
  discarded
1 litre (4 cups) water
2 tablespoons black soy
  sauce
1 tablespoon
  Worcestershire sauce
1 teaspoon salt
3–4 potatoes, (400 g/
  13 oz), cut in chunks
2 carrots, sliced diagonally
Celery leaves, to garnish
  (optional)
Freshly ground black
  pepper, to taste

1 Heat the oil in a large saucepan and add the garlic and onions. Stir-fry over medium heat until they soften, then add the cinnamon, star anise, cloves and peppercorns. Stir-fry for 2 minutes, then add the oxtail, water, soy sauce, Worcestershire sauce and salt. Bring to a boil, cover, lower the heat and simmer until just tender, 1–1 1/4 hours. If you wish to remove the fat, strain the stock and put the meat and spices in a covered container. Allow the stock to cool, then put in the deep-freeze until the fat sets on the top. Skim off and discard the fat.

2 Return the stock and oxtail to the pan. Add the potatoes and carrots, bring to a boil, cover and simmer until the meat and vegetables are soft, 15–20 minutes.

3 Sprinkle with freshly ground black pepper, then serve with crusty French bread and green vegetables.

Serves 4
Preparation time: **15 mins + 1 hour chilling (optional)**
Cooking time: **1 1/2–1 3/4 hours**

Fragrant Beef Stew (Smoore)

This Dutch-influenced dish (also known as *semur* or *smoore*) is found in different versions in Sri Lanka, Malacca, Singapore and Indonesia. Some recipes call for the beef to be cooked in one piece and sliced at the table, like a Dutch pot roast. Although Sri Lanka's Burghers use coconut milk instead of water, other Eurasians rely on spices and sauces for flavour.

750 g (1^1/$_2$ lbs) topside beef, cubed
2 tablespoons vinegar
2 tablespoons black soy sauce
2 teaspoons peppercorns, crushed
2 teaspoons coriander seeds, crushed
1 teaspoon sugar
2 cloves garlic, minced
2 tablespoons oil
2 cinnamon sticks, each 8 cm (3^1/$_4$ in) long
2 star anise pods
4 cloves
2 onions, halved and thinly sliced
2 teaspoons grated ginger
1 teaspoon salt
2–3 cups (500–750 ml) water
2–3 potatoes, (400 g/ 13 oz) quartered
2 tablespoons fresh breadcrumbs

1 Place the beef in a bowl and sprinkle with the vinegar, soy sauce, pepper, coriander, sugar and garlic. Rub well with the hands and set aside to marinate for at least 15 minutes.

2 Heat the oil in a saucepan and stir-fry the cinnamon, star anise and cloves for 1 minute. Add the onions and ginger and stir-fry over medium heat until the onions turn golden. Add the marinated beef and stir-fry until it changes colour. Add the salt and just enough water to cover. Bring to a boil, cover, lower the heat and simmer until the beef is tender, about 1 hour.

3 Add the potatoes and continue simmering until the potatoes are cooked, adding a little more water if needed to ensure the potatoes cook properly. Stir in the breadcrumbs to thicken the sauce, then serve hot.

Serves 4
Preparation time: 15 mins + 15 mins marinating
Cooking time: 1^3/$_4$–2 hours

Gammon Curry

This unusual recipe combines Indian spices with Portuguese ingredients such as wine vinegar, olive oil, prunes and green olives. Although not a common dish, it is an excellent example of the creativity of Eurasian cooks. Be sure to use whole spices for maximum flavour.

1 tablespoon cumin seeds
8–10 dried chillies,
   cut in lengths, soaked
   in hot water to soften,
   drained
2 tablespoons olive oil
85–125 ml ($^1/_3$–$^1/_2$ cup)
   red wine vinegar
500 g (1 lb) gammon or
   lean back bacon, cubed
$^1/_4$ teaspoon fenugreek
   seeds
$^1/_2$ teaspoon brown
   mustard seeds
10–12 curry leaves
$^1/_2$ cup pitted prunes
8 green olives
Sugar to taste (optional)

Serves 4
Preparation time: **15 mins**
 + 2 hours marinating
Cooking time: **1–1$^1/_4$ hours**

1 Dry-roast the cumin seeds in a pan over low heat for 1 minute until fragrant. Process the cumin seeds to a powder in a spice grinder. Add the chillies and process until smooth. Heat 1 tablespoon of the oil in a small saucepan, then stir-fry the chilli mixture over low heat for 4 minutes. Transfer to a bowl and stir in the vinegar, mixing well. Add the meat, stir and marinate for 2 hours at room temperature.

2 Heat the remaining oil in a saucepan and add the fenugreek, mustard seeds and curry leaves. Stir-fry over medium heat for about 1 minute, taking care not to brown the fenugreek.

3 Drain the meat, reserving the marinade. Add the meat to the spices in the pan and stir-fry until the meat changes colour and the juices have dried up, 6–8 minutes. Add the reserved marinade and water to just cover the meat. Bring to a boil, cover and simmer until the meat is tender, 30–45 minutes.

4 Add the prunes and olives and simmer, covered, for 10 minutes. Taste and add sugar, if desired. Serve hot with steamed white rice.

Minced Meat with Fried Potatoes

This very English-sounding recipe dates from the mid-19th century, when unrest in China forced the Portuguese and Macanese to take refuge in Hong Kong for a short period. Macanese cooks obviously picked up a few cooking methods and ingredients from the British, incorporating these with familiar Chinese ingredients such as wood fungus and soy sauce. This mild dish is sure to appeal to everyone.

Oil for deep-frying
2 large potatoes, diced
  and dried with paper
  towels
2 tablespoons lard or oil
2 onions, diced
2 cloves garlic, minced
250 g (8 oz) minced
  pork
250 g (8 oz) minced
  beef
$1/4$ cup dried wood ear
  fungus, soaked, hard
  portions discarded,
  chopped
$1^1/_2$ tablespoons black
  soy sauce
2 teaspoons sugar
125 ml ($1/_2$ cup) water
$1/_2$ teaspoon salt or more
  to taste
$1/_2$ teaspoon freshly
  ground black pepper
Sprig of parsley or coriander leaves to garnish
  (optional)

1 Heat the oil in a wok until very hot. Add the diced potato and fry until golden brown and tender, 4–5 minutes. Remove and drain. Remove the oil from the wok.
2 Add the lard or fresh oil to the wok. Heat until moderately hot, then add the onion and stir-fry until transparent, 3–4 minutes. Increase the heat and add the pork and beef. Stir-fry until the meat changes colour, 2–3 minutes. Add the fungus, soy sauce, sugar, water, salt and pepper. Bring to a boil, lower the heat and simmer uncovered until the meat is cooked and the liquid has dried up, about 15 minutes. The meat can be kept at room temperature for 1–2 hours before finishing the dish.
3 Just before serving, heat the meat and add the fried potatoes. Cook over moderate heat, stirring gently so the potatoes do not break up, until heated through, 2 minutes. Garnish with a sprig of parsley or coriander leaves, if using, and serve with plain white rice.

Serves 4
Preparation time: **10 mins**
Cooking time: **15 mins**

Feng

250 g (8 oz) pork liver

1 pork kidney or 2 lamb kidneys, halved

250 g (8 oz) ox tripe, (optional)

1 tablespoon baking powder

250 g (8 oz) ox tongue,

250 g (8 oz) topside beef

250 g (8 oz) belly pork, with skin

2 tablespoons olive oil

3 cm ($1^1/_4$ in) cinnamon

1 whole star anise

4 cloves

1 teaspoon salt

$^1/_4$ teaspoon freshly grated nutmeg

2–3 potatoes, (400 g/ 13 oz), cubed

2 onions, each cut in wedges

60–125 ml ($^1/_4$–$^1/_2$ cup) red wine vinegar

1 tablespoon chopped Chinese celery leaves or fresh coriander leaves

Marinade

4 tablespoons coriander seeds

2 tablespoons cumin

1 tablespoon black peppercorns

1 tablespoon fennel

$^1/_2$ teaspoon turmeric powder

20 shallots

3 cm (1in)ginger

8–10 cloves garlic

3 tablespoons sweet sherry

1 To prepare the Marinade, heat the coriander seeds, cumin, pepper and fennel in a small pan, shaking frequently, until the spices become fragrant and are just starting to change colour, about 1 minute. Grind to a fine powder in a spice grinder and transfer to a bowl. Process the shallots, ginger and garlic to a smooth paste, adding a little of the sherry if needed to keep the mixture turning. Add to the spices and mix well.

2 Rinse the liver and kidneys in water and remove the white membranes from the kidneys with a sharp knife. Drop the liver and kidneys into boiling water for 1 minute to firm slightly, then set aside. Soak the tripe, if using, and kidneys in 1 tablespoon of baking powder for 30 minutes, then drop them in boiling water for about 10 minutes and set aside. Clean and scrape the ox tongue thoroughly, then drop in boiling water for about 10 minutes and set aside. Cut all the meats into small cubes then add to the Marinade, mixing well with your fingers. Cover and leave to marinate (in the refrigerator if weather is hot) for 2 hours.

3 Heat the oil in an earthenware, stainless steel or enamelled saucepan and add the cinnamon, star anise and cloves. Stir-fry for 2 minutes, then add the meat and its Marinade and stir-fry until all the liquid dries up. Add the salt, nutmeg and sufficient water to cover the meat.

4 Bring to a boil, cover, lower the heat and simmer until the meat is just cooked, about 45 minutes. Add the potatoes and onion and simmer for 10 minutes. Add vinegar to taste and cook until the potatoes are soft. Serve garnished with Chinese celery or coriander leaves and with plain rice or a pilau.

An alternative to cleaning the kidneys and tripe in baking powder is to rub salt into the meat and rinse it off. This helps rid the meat of any odours.

Serves 6–8
Preparation time: **20 mins + 2 hours marinating**
Cooking time: **2 hours**

Lamb Chops with Black Pepper Sauce

The Eurasians of Singapore and Malaysia happily borrow ingredients and cooking styles from other ethnic communities. This recipe for lamb is a good example, mixing Indian spices such as cardamom with Southeast Asian cinnamon and cloves, Chinese oyster and soy sauce, with lashings of black pepper and garlic.

$1/4$ cup (60 ml) black soy sauce

2 tablespoons oyster sauce

1 tablespoon oil

1 tablespoon minced garlic

2 tablespoons coarsely crushed peppercorns

6 cardamom pods, slit and bruised, or $1/2$ teaspoon cardamom powder

4 cloves

8 cm (3 in) cinnamon stick

$1/2$–$3/4$cup (125–185 ml) water

8 lamb chops, (600–800g /$1 1/2$–2 lbs) excess fat trimmed

1 tablespoon sugar

1 small onion, thinly sliced, rings separated

180 g (1 cup) cooked green peas

1 Combine the soy sauce and oyster sauce in a small bowl and set aside. Heat the oil in a large frying pan. Add the garlic, pepper, cardamom, cloves and cinnamon and stir-fry over medium heat until fragrant, about 30 seconds. Add the sauce mixture and stir for 30 seconds. 2 Add the water and bring to a boil, stirring. Add the lamb chops and simmer uncovered over medium heat for 5–8 minutes until the meat is tender, turning the chops a couple of times. Add the sugar, onion and green peas. Stir for 1 minute over medium heat, then transfer to a serving dish and serve hot.

Serves 4
Preparation time: **10 mins**
Cooking time: **15 mins**

Fried Pork Chops

1 tablespoon sugar
2 teaspoons thick black
soy sauce
2 teaspoons soy sauce
1 teaspoon rice wine
1 teaspoon grated ginger
$^{1}/_{2}$ teaspoon salt
$^{1}/_{4}$ teaspoon white pepper
4 pork chops
10 unsweetened cream
cracker biscuits, crushed
like coarse bread crumbs
$^{1}/_{3}$ cup (40 g) self-raising
flour
2 eggs, lightly beaten
Oil for shallow-frying
Cherry tomatoes and
cucumber slices to
garnish (optional)

1 Put the sugar, and both soy sauces with the wine, ginger, salt and pepper in a bowl, stirring to dissolve the sugar.
2 Put the chops in a single layer in a wide dish and spread with half of the marinade. Turn the chops over and spread with the remaining marinade. Leave for 30 minutes, turning once or twice. Combine the cracker crumbs and flour in a shallow bowl. Put the egg in another shallow bowl.
3 One at a time, drain a chop then dip in the egg. Drain again then press both sides into the cracker mix. Dip in egg again then in the cracker mix so each chop is coated twice. Repeat with the remaining chops.
4 Heat 1 cm ($^{1}/_{2}$ in) oil in a frying pan, add the chops and fry over high heat, turning to brown on both sides and cook through. Drain on paper towels. Garnish with tomatoes and cucumber.

Serves 4
Preparation time: **15 mins + 30 mins marinating**
Cooking time: **10–12 mins**

Spicy Tomato Sambal

1 tablespoon oil
1 small onion, chopped
1 clove garlic, minced
1 1/2 teaspoons Chinese
  shrimp sauce
1/2 teaspoon turmeric
  powder
2 ripe tomatoes, peeled
  and chopped (see note)
2 tablespoons coconut
  cream
1/2–1 teaspoon chilli
  powder
1/2 teaspoon salt
1/4 teaspoon sugar

Serves 4
Preparation time: **10 mins**
Cooking time: **20–25 mins**

1 Heat the oil in a saucepan and stir-fry the onion and garlic over low-medium heat until soft. Add the shrimp paste and turmeric and stir-fry over medium heat until fragrant, 1–2 minutes.

2 Add the tomatoes, coconut cream, chilli powder, salt and sugar. Bring to a boil, stirring several times, then simmer uncovered, stirring occasionally, until the mixture is quite thick, 10–15 minutes.

3 This sambal can be served together with rice, a meat or poultry dish, and a green vegetable or salad.

To peel the tomatoes, dip them in rapidly boiling water for 15–20 seconds. Put under running water until cool enough to handle. Use a sharp knife to remove core, then slip off the skin.

Mixed Vegetable and Stuffed Chilli Pickles

350 g (12 oz) unripe green papaya or daikon radish (lobak), very finely shredded
2 tablespoons coarse salt
16 shallots, pricked all over with a fork
10 green beans, cut diagonally in pieces
1 small cucumber, quartered lengthwise, deseeded, flesh sliced
100 g (1 cup) cauliflower, florets
100 g (1$^1/_4$ cup) cabbage, coarsely chopped
5 cm (2 in) ginger, very finely sliced
4 cloves garlic, thinly sliced lengthwise
6 large green chillies

Pickling Mixture
1 teaspoon brown mustard seed
3 tablespoons dried prawns, soaked in warm water to soften, drained
1 teaspoon turmeric powder
2 teaspoons dried shrimp paste
2 cloves garlic, chopped
3 tablespoons oil
500 ml (2 cups) distilled white vinegar
200 g ($^3/_4$ cup + 1 tablespoon) sugar
1 teaspoon salt

1 If possible, shred the papaya on a mandolin so that the shreds are very thin. Put the papaya in a bowl and sprinkle with 2 teaspoons salt. Toss well then put on a basket tray and dry in the sun until completely dry, about 2 days. Alternatively, spread on an oven tray and dry in an oven set at the lowest possible heat until the papaya is dry and crisp.

2 Place the shallots, beans, cucumber, cauliflower and cabbage in a bowl and sprinkle with 1 tablespoon salt, tossing to mix well. Combine the garlic and ginger in a separate bowl, sprinkle with 1 teaspoon of the salt, and toss to mix well. Put all the salted ingredients on a basket tray and dry in the sun until limp, 2–3 hours, or dry in an oven set on lowest possible heat for 1 hour.

3 To make the Pickling Mixture, blend or pound the mustard seeds until fine, then add the dried prawns and blend until fine. Add the turmeric, shrimp paste and garlic and process to a smooth paste, adding a little of the oil if needed to keep the mixture turning. Heat the oil in a saucepan and fry the blended mixture over medium heat until fragrant, about 5 minutes, then add the vinegar, sugar and salt and bring almost to a boil. Remove from the heat.

4 Trim the stalks from each chilli but leave on the stem. Make a lengthwise slit along one side of each chilli, from the stalk to the tip, taking care not to cut through. Use the tip of a sharp knife to remove the seeds and membranes from inside each chilli, then insert some of the dried papaya, pressing firmly.

5 Place the dried vegetables and stuffed chillies into a large jar, packing them firmly. Bring the Pickling Mixture back to a boil, then pour it over the vegetables. Allow to cool, then close the jar and store for at least 3 days before serving. Will keep up to 6 months if refrigerated.

Serves 4
Preparation time: **1 hour + 2 days sun drying**
Cooking time: **10 mins**

Salted Fish Pickle

Salted fish — a standby from the days of sailing boats, when it was dangerous to go to in search of fresh fish during the monsoons — is still very popular among Eurasians in Singapore and Malacca; a similar version (known as Para) is also made in Goa.

300 g (10 oz) salted fish (such as *ikan kurau* or *ikan mergui*)
125 ml ($^1/_2$ cup) oil
1 tablespoon coriander powder
1 tablespoon cumin powder
1 teaspoon fennel powder
1 teaspoon turmeric
250 ml (1 cup) white vinegar
3 tablespoons grated ginger
6–8 cloves garlic, minced
6–8 shallots, or 1 medium red onion, chopped
10–12 dried chillies, cut in lengths, soaked in hot water until soft, drained
3–4 tablespoons sugar

1 Rinse the fish briefly, then put in the sun or in an oven set to very low heat until completely dry. Cut into 1-cm ($^1/_2$-in) slices. Heat the oil in a wok and add the salted fish. Fry over medium heat, stirring frequently, until the fish is golden brown all over and crisp, about 5 minutes. Drain the fish on paper towels, leaving the oil in the wok.

2 Combine the coriander, cumin, fennel and turmeric with about $1^1/_2$ tablespoons of the vinegar to make a paste. Set aside. Process the ginger, garlic, shallots and chillies in a spice grinder until they form a smooth paste.

3 Heat the oil left in the wok and add the spice mixture and chilli paste. Stir-fry over low–medium heat until cooked and the oil starts to separate, about 10 minutes. Add the remaining vinegar and sugar to taste and cook for 1 minute, stirring until the sugar dissolves. Add the fried salted fish, stir, then transfer to a jar.

4 When cool, cover the jar and store 1 week before using. Serve with rice and other dishes. Keeps up to 6 months if refrigerated.

Serves 4
Preparation time: **20 mins (excludes drying of fish)**
Cooking time: **20 mins**

Pineapple Tarts

190 g (1½ cups) flour
Pinch of salt
90 g (4½ tablespoons) chilled butter,
1 egg
1 teaspoon lemon juice
2 egg whites
Whole cloves for topping (optional)
30 tartlet trays

Filling

1 small ripe pineapple, (800–900 g /1¾–2 lbs), peeled, cored and chopped
160 g (1 cup) soft brown sugar, or more to taste
1 tablespoon lemon juice
3 cloves
2 star anise petals
Few gratings of nutmeg

Makes 30 tarts
Preparation time: **10 mins**
Cooking time: **25 mins**

1 Make the Filling by processing the pineapple in a food processor or blender until coarsely crushed, about 10 seconds. Transfer to a saucepan with a heavy base, or a non-stick saucepan. Add the sugar, lemon juice, cloves, star anise and nutmeg. Simmer uncovered over medium–high heat until thick, stirring frequently with a wooden spoon, about 20–25 minutes. Transfer to a shallow bowl and allow to cool. Remove the whole spices.

2 Put the flour, salt and butter into a food processor and pulse until the mixture resembles breadcrumbs. Add the egg and lemon juice and process until it forms a ball. Put in a plastic bag and refrigerate 30 minutes.

3 Roll out the dough very thinly on a floured board. Use a cutter to cut out 30 circles, each 6 cm (2½ in) in diameter. Press into well-greased tartlet trays, fluting up the edges with pastry cuttes or a fork. Fill each pastry with 1 teaspoon pineapple jam. Brush with egg white and top with a clove, if desired.

4 Bake at 180°C (350°F) until golden brown, about 20 minutes. Remove from the oven, loosen the tarts with a knife and transfer to racks to cool. Store in an airtight container when completely cooled.

This recipe results in light, firm and crispy tarts. Another alternative to fluting the edges of the pastry is to cut the dough with a cookie cutter that has scalloped or serrated edges. Then, push each piece of dough into a cupcake tray to shape it.

Cinnamon, Nutmeg and Coconut Layer Cake

Known in Goa as *bebinca*, this method for making this recipe is similar to the Dutch-influenced layer cake or *kueh lapis* of Indonesia, and also to the *bebinca* of Macau, although the latter uses rice flour. The cake tastes like a soft, steamed pudding and is not oily or creamy. It is excellent served as a dessert.

125 g ($^1/_2$ cup) caster sugar
5 egg yolks
100 g ($^2/_3$ cup) flour, sifted
375 ml ($1^1/_2$ cups) thick coconut milk
3 tablespoons butter, melted
Freshly grated nutmeg
Cinnamon powder
Vanilla icecream

Serves 4
Preparation time: 15 mins
Cooking time: About
   1 hour (5 mins per layer)

1 Beat the sugar and egg yolks together until the sugar has completely dissolved, then stir in the flour. Gradually stir in the coconut milk, mixing to combine thoroughly.
2 Dip a brush in the melted butter and paint the sides of a small, deep cake pan about 15 cm (6 in) in diameter, or a loaf tin about 18 x 8 cm (7 x 3 in). Pour in two or three ladles of batter to make a thin layer about 4 cm ($1^1/_2$ in) thick.
3 Sprinkle the top liberally with nutmeg and cinnamon. Set the cake pan in a baking dish of hot water and bake in a moderate oven 180°C (350°F) until just set, about 5 minutes. Remove the cake pan from the oven and brush the top of the cooked layer with melted butter. Pour in more batter to make another thin layer and sprinkle with nutmeg and cinnamon. Return to the oven and cook until set.
4 Repeat until the batter is used up, brushing the top of each newly cooked layer with butter before adding the batter and spices.
5 When the last layer has cooked, remove from the oven and allow to cool in the pan. When cooled, loosen the edges with a knife and turn the cake upside down onto a serving plate. Serve chilled with a scoop of vanilla icecream.

Semolina Cake (Sugee)

Cake made with semolina or *sugee*, is popular in many Eurasian communities. In Sri Lanka, the Burghers call it Love Cake and add cashew nuts, rose essence and cardamom. In Malaysia and Singapore, almonds replace the cashews and the flavouring is usually vanilla, a touch of brandy and lemon rind. Here is the Sri Lankan version.

250 g (8 oz) butter, softened
250 g (1$^1/_2$ cups) fine semolina
7 eggs, separated
250 g (1 cup) caster sugar
2 tablespoons rose water or $^1/_2$ teaspoon rose essence
$^1/_2$ teaspoon freshly grated nutmeg
$^1/_2$ teaspoon cardamom powder, preferably freshly ground
$^1/_2$ teaspoon finely grated lemon rind
250 g (1$^3/_4$ cups) raw cashew nuts, coarsely chopped
125 g (1 cup) flour

Serves 8–10
Preparation time: **20 mins + 1 hour soaking**
Cooking time: **1 hour**

1 Grease and line a 20-cm (8-in) square cake pan with 2 layers of baking paper, brushing the inside of the second layer with melted butter.
2 Put the butter in a bowl and use a wooden spoon to gradually stir in the semolina. Beat firmly for about 1 minute, then leave the semolina to soften for 1 hour.
3 Put the egg yolks in a bowl and beat with an electric beater, gradually adding the sugar to make a light, creamy mixture. Stir in the rose essence, nutmeg, cardamom and lemon rind, mixing well, then use a spatula to fold in the butter and semolina. When this is thoroughly mixed, fold in the cashews and flour. Beat the egg whites until they hold firm peaks, then carefully fold one-third at a time into the mixture.
4 Transfer to the prepared cake pan and bake at 150°C (300°F) until the cake is golden brown and feels firm to the touch, about 1 hour (do not pierce the cake to test if cooked or it may collapse). If the cake starts to brown too quickly, cover the top loosely with foil.
5 Remove the cooked cake from the oven and leave in the pan until completely cooled. Remove the cake from the pan, leaving the paper attached. Cut into slices to serve and transfer to a serving plate. Store any leftover cake in a covered container.

Index